SPECTRUM®
READERS

ASTOUNDING!
Asian
Animals

By Lisa Kurkov

 Carson-Dellosa
Publishing

SPECTRUM®

An imprint of Carson-Dellosa Publishing, LLC
P.O. Box 35665
Greensboro, NC 27425-5665

carsondellosa.com

Printed in the USA. All rights reserved.
ISBN 978-1-4838-0132-2

01-002141120

Asia is the largest continent on Earth. No wonder it has such a variety of animals!

Animals in Russia are prepared for snow. Animals in Iran are used to the desert. Asian animals are as interesting as the places where they make their homes.

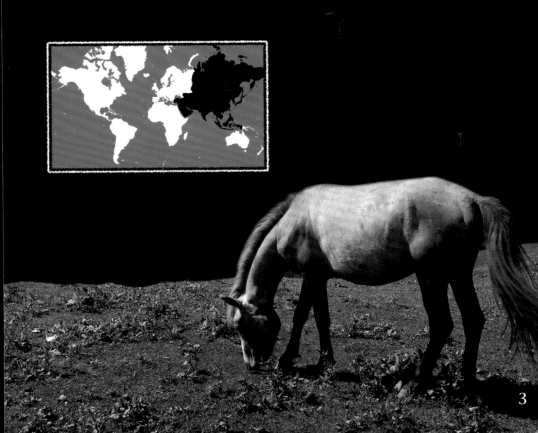

Giant Panda

Giant pandas live high up in the mountains of China.
This is the only place in the world where wild pandas are found.
Pandas eat bamboo . . . lots of it!
They eat 20 to 40 pounds a day of this coarse grass.
Pandas are an endangered species.
Only about 1,600 remain in the wild.

Fun Facts

- A mother panda is about 900 times bigger than her baby!

- The Chinese name for panda means "large bear-cat."

6

Red Panda

Red pandas are much smaller than their cousins the giant pandas.
Scientists used to group them with bears.
Then, scientists placed these unique animals in a class with raccoons.
Today, red pandas are in a class by themselves.
Like giant pandas, red pandas eat bamboo and live high in trees.

Fun Facts

- *Lesser panda* is another name for the red panda.
- Red pandas wrap their long tails around themselves to keep warm.

Bengal Tiger

Asia is home to several kinds of big cats.
The Bengal tiger lives in India.
Like most big cats, it lives alone.
Tigers' beautiful stripes camouflage them
in the forest.
This allows them to sneak up on prey.
Bengal tigers feed on large mammals like
deer, pigs, and antelope.
Tigers sometimes save meat for later.
They bury it under leaves and dirt.

Fun Facts

- No two tigers have exactly the same stripes!
- Tigers like to swim and enjoy the water.

Siberian Tiger

Siberian tigers are the largest cats.
They can weigh up to 700 pounds—about
as much as a motorcycle!
Most live in the cold forests of Russia.
At night, they roam long distances across
the tundra to find prey.
Elk and wild boar are favorite meals.
These powerful tigers can kill with one
pounce.

Fun Facts

- Tigers mark their scent on trees. This
  tells other tigers to stay away.
- A tiger has two to six cubs at a time.

Caracal

Caracals are medium-sized wild cats.
An adult weighs about as much as a
preschool child.
They live in the Middle East and India.
Caracals have unique ear tufts or tassels.
Scientists think the cats may use their
tufts to communicate.
Caracals are amazing jumpers.
They can leap up to heights of 10 feet!

Fun Facts

- Another name for the caracal is *desert lynx*.

- The name *caracal* comes from a Turkish word that means "black ear."

13

Snow Leopard

Snow leopards live high in the mountains of Central Asia.

Their thick coats keep them warm in harsh winter weather.

Some prey on farm animals.

This upsets farmers, who sometimes kill snow leopards.

They are also hunted for their coats.

Conservation groups help to protect snow leopards.

Fun Facts

- Snow leopards' fur can grow more than five inches long!
- Snow leopards can't roar. They make a puffing sound called a *chuff*.

Clouded Leopard

Clouded leopards make their homes in tropical forests.
They are excellent climbers.
They can even hang upside down from tree branches!
Their long tails help them balance.
Clouded leopards are rare.
Scientists have not had many chances to watch them in the wild.
They can learn a lot by observing the leopards in zoos.

Fun Facts

- A group of clouded leopards is called a *leap*.
- Clouded leopards get their name from the cloud-like spots on their fur.

Sambar Deer

Sambar deer are large hoofed mammals.
They live in India and Southeast Asia.
Sambar deer are *nocturnal*, which means
they are active at night.
Their diet is made of grasses, vines,
shrubs, and fruit.
Males grow large antlers with six
projections called *points*.
They shed their antlers once a year.

- Sambar deer like to visit natural salt licks.
- Tigers and leopards prey on sambar deer.

Asian Elephant

Asian elephants live in tropical forests. An adult male can weigh 11,000 pounds! Even though they are big, their wide, padded feet allow them to walk silently through the forest.

These giants are herbivores that eat leaves, grasses, fruit, and bark. Elephants live in herds and groups of herds, called *clans*.

Fun Facts

- An elephant has more than 40,000 muscles in its trunk alone!
- Females are pregnant for 22 months— nearly two years.

Macaque

Japanese macaques are also commonly called *snow monkeys*.
In winter, they take baths in hot springs.
Macaques are very smart, and they learn new things from each other.
Knowledge is passed from one generation to the next.
This may be how some macaques learned to rinse their food in salt water.
It cleans food and makes it taste good!

Fun Facts

- In winter, macaques play in the snow and make snowballs.
- Macaques live further north than any other primate—except humans!

King Cobra

King cobras are huge, and they can be fierce predators.

These snakes can grow to 18 feet in length—the size of three adult men!

A king cobra has a hood around its head that opens when the animal feels threatened.

King cobras don't often attack humans. They feed on other snakes, lizards, eggs, and small mammals.

Fun Facts

- The venom in one king cobra bite could kill 20 people!

- King cobras spend time in trees, on land, and in water.

Komodo Dragon

Strange-looking Komodo dragons live only in Indonesia.
At weights up to 300 pounds, they are the biggest and heaviest lizards on Earth.
Komodo dragons eat deer, pigs, other lizards, and even water buffalo!
Their saliva (spit) is high in bacteria.
If their bite does not kill an animal, their saliva will!

Fun Facts

- Komodo dragons can wait hours for prey to come by.
- They use their forked tongues to help them "smell" other animals.

Camel

Both types of camels, Bactrian and Arabian, are found in Asia.
Arabian camels have one hump, and Bactrian camels have two.
These desert animals store fat in their amazing humps.
This allows camels to go for long stretches without food or water.
People use camels as pack animals.
Today, almost all camels are domestic (not wild) animals.

Fun Facts

- Camels rarely sweat, allowing them to conserve water.
- Camels can close their nostrils to keep sand out.

Brown Bear

Brown bears are found throughout Asia. Their powerful shoulder muscles form a "hump" on their backs.

For nearly half the year, they feast on insects, berries, grass, fruit, and fish.

For the other half of the year, they hibernate in dens hidden in rocks or dug under tree roots.

Mothers give birth inside the dens.

Fun Facts

- Brown bears use long, sharp claws to find insects in logs.
- During hibernation, a bear's heart rate may drop from 40 to 8 beats a minute.

31

ASTOUNDING! Asian Animals Comprehension Questions

1. What do giant pandas eat?

2. Where do red pandas live?

3. What is the purpose of a tiger's stripes?

4. Where do Siberian tigers live?

5. Why do scientists think caracals have tufts on their ears?

6. Give two reasons why snow leopards are hunted.

7. Why do some macaques rinse their food in salt water?

8. Why do you think scientists have trouble finding clouded leopards in the wild?

9. What does it mean that sambar deer are nocturnal?

10. When does a king cobra's hood open?

For a complete reading experience, be sure to read all of the Level 3 Spectrum Readers!

For more information, visit
carsondellosa.com/spectrum

CD-704420

Bring real-world topics to life with Spectrum Readers!

This high-interest, nonfiction reading series provides young learners an opportunity to explore interesting, informational reading topics on their own. Nonfiction readers are an important resource for engaging children while building knowledge and developing reading skills. Children will love to learn with Spectrum Readers!

Level 1: Beginning to Read

Level 2: Reading with Help

Level 3: Reading Alone

Level 3 Readers are the perfect start for children who are beginning to read multisyllable words and more complex sentences on their own.

**An imprint of
Carson-Dellosa Publishing LLC**

U.S. $3.99

ISBN: 978-1-4838-0132-2
50399

9 781483 801322

carsondellosa.com/spectrum
Guided Reading Level: K

0 44222 23376 1

EAN